GW00640788

Living With Him

Everything you need to know

Alex Hallatt

summersdale

Living With Him

Summersdale Publishers Ltd
46 West Street
Chichester
West Sussex
PO19 1RP
UK

www.summersdale.com

Printed and bound in Belgium

ISBN 1 84024 448 8

For Gary – my inspiration

Contents

INTRODUCTION

Congratulations: you've found one of the decent ones. He's passed the initial screening, stayed the distance and is committed enough to want to move in with you. No more commuting to see each other, unless it's from the bathroom to the bedroom.

But seeing more of each other doesn't necessarily mean you get more of what you had before. Living together is an exciting transition, but a big one too and not something for the ill-prepared. Reading this book will make the change less hit and miss and more a case of domestic bliss.

PRACTICALITIES

NUTRITION

Blokes consider there to be four major food groups: beer, meat, cheese and chips. This will be self-evident if you pack him off to the supermarket. Men don't like to follow lists, so sending him shopping will be futile if you really need something.

You will now find he was humouring you when he said he ate a lot of fruit. He actually meant raspberry ice cream, mango chutney and the limes in his Corona. His idea of a balanced diet is to eat multivitamins.

Following recipes is as much of an affront to his masculinity as asking for directions.

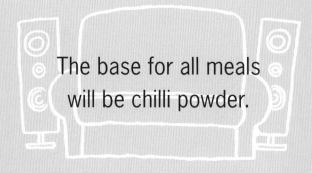

The base for all meals will be chilli powder.

If you go away for a holiday with the girls, don't be surprised to come back to find the rubbish bin overflowing with pizza and ready meal boxes.

Any veggies that you suggested he use up will now be a slimy mess of goop stuck to the bottom of the fridge crisper drawer.

HOUSEWORK
Cleaning

A man's hunter-gatherer instinct does not extend to cleaning – if he can't see dirt, it's not there. Therefore there is no need to clean underneath the bed, on top of the cupboards, or the back of the fridge. Ever.

You would be mortified to leave skid marks in the loo, but it is a source of pride to your man.

Men think that bathrooms are self-cleaning because they have running water in them.

Men regard cleaning as a nancy thing to do, unless using industrial strength bleach, sprayed with abandon from a distance. Look out for mysterious tie-dye patterns appearing on your new Prada blouse.

Tidying

Before you lived together you knew where everything was. Now things will go missing for ages and reappear at random: mugs growing mouldy underneath the bed, tea towels in the greenhouse and the remote control in the bathroom.

He will get annoyed if you tidy
any of his things away.

He will still expect you to know where his keys/phone/wallet are, one minute before he has to leave the house.

Laundry

Men do not read labels or realise there is more than one setting on the washing machine. Safeguard anything that cannot be boil-washed.

Washing-up

If you cook and he washes up, don't criticise his technique; if you have to, surreptitiously re-wash everything later.

Otherwise you might need to get used to the taste of dishwashing liquid in your cups of tea.

HOME IMPROVEMENTS

Now you have moved in together, you can work on creating your dream home, right? Well, yes, if your dream home includes a manly brown colour scheme and a massive home entertainment system with surround sound and a sofa able to accommodate a dozen mates when the game's on…

... If not, expect a lot of arguments and compromises. This is why so many couples' homes end up magnolia, as it is the least offensive colour to both men and women.

Two words make DIY appealing to men and they aren't 'colour coordination'. To really get your man's pulse racing just utter the magic words 'power tools'.

Insider's tip: Get your own toolbox and hide it away somewhere he won't find it (e.g. the bed linen cupboard). That way, you'll be able to find a screwdriver when you need one and, in the eventuality of having to split up, you won't be left without one.

For anything more complicated than decorating, get the professionals in. Your man may think that he can put in a new bathroom, but are you prepared...

... for it to take nearly as long as it took for you to agree to live together?

... to rush him to hospital when he has a nasty accident with a tile-cutter?

... for water to leak through the badly grouted tiles into the electrics of the new kitchen lighting system that you only just got fixed after his last job?

Men don't want to spend money on furniture when they think that, with the right tools, they can make their own.

Unless you put a stop to this, you will have an empty joint account, a shed full of power tools and a bum full of splinters.

MONEY

Living together may mean he trusts you enough to know the PIN to his bankcard. You shouldn't abuse this trust. Even if he forgets your birthday and the fact you really wanted him to get you some new underwear that you know he'd love too. You really shouldn't. Well, maybe on this occasion… oh, go on then…

Other, less generous, men will demand that a housekeeping book is used to keep track of expenses. You will need to employ creative accounting: put lunch with friends under the heading 'food shopping'; clothes under 'cleaning rags' (some day they might be); and bottles of Bollinger under 'fizzy drink'.

The money in a joint account isn't free. He won't be best pleased if you buy a place together and the mortgage payments bounce because of a series of impulse buys at Harvey Nicks.

Financial independence can stop you feeling trapped when you are living with someone. Consider having an emergency escape fund, even if it is just the bus fare to your mother's place.

Hiding the phone bill from him
won't make it smaller.

YOUR RELATIONSHIP

SEX AND ROMANCE

Living together may not spell the end of romance, but your man may redefine it in the following ways:

🏠 Using banana-flavoured condoms because you said you liked fruit.

🏠 Putting the sports channel on mute if you have set the table for the anniversary dinner you cooked.

🏠 Surprising you with a weekend away... to a place that just happens to be hosting the Cup final.

🏠 Eating most of the chocolates he bought you for Valentine's Day so you don't get fat.

🏠 Running you a bath by using only the hot water tap so that you scald yourself when blindly clambering in through the steam.

🏠 Buying you sexy lingerie... that's two sizes too small.

Living together should mean sex on tap, any time you want it, but you'll have to learn to co-ordinate those desires. Otherwise, your nudges may be met with 'after I've beaten my high score on this computer game, honey' and 'didn't we do that last week?'.

Remember that sex is still a special thing and not something that should be interrupted for:

🏠 putting the rubbish out

🏠 a repeated episode of *Friends*

🏠 a phone call from your mother

🏠 preservation of the clean sheets
   you only changed that week

Repetition in anything can get dull, so vary position and location. Logically there are only so many options when you are living under the same roof, so you may have to use friends' places, make the most of a bad movie or even enjoy public transport.

CONVERSATION

Don't believe him when he says he can listen to you and watch TV at the same time. Men don't multi-task.

Men are not mind readers and are unlikely to know that you have been worrying about something for weeks before you bring the subject up with them. If he has noticed this, make sure he isn't gay.

If he is angry, talking about it will not make him feel better.

Furthermore, try not to bring any arguments into the bedroom. He is likely to feign sleep to get off the hook.

Picking Saturday's big game as the perfect moment to talk to him can work for you as well as against you (see first point). He might well agree with anything you say just to get you to leave him alone. This is great if you are asking if you can throw out his porn collection, but not such a good idea if you expect a definitive answer to whether he wants to spend the rest of his life with you.

In fact, there is never a good time to talk to him about anything of importance to you – unless you have a serious interest in car engine specifications, sports statistics or whether the woman next door has had cosmetic surgery on her breasts.

GUIDELINES

TERRITORY
The Television

Never mind that he changes channels quicker than you can say 'But I like *Sex and the City*!' Let him have the remote – it gives him a sense of power and control over his world. It will be to your advantage if you learn to program the video recorder, as this is likely to be a mystery to him.

58

Answerphone

You have to include his name in the message, even if you are the only one who ever answers the phone.

The Bedroom

Farting in bed is his way of marking his territory.

The Smallest Room in the Home

Even if you cook together and eat the same meals, he will spend longer on the loo than you. This is a biological mystery.

Men need to have personal space for time to contemplate or, perhaps, read. Their meditative spot of choice involves a hard wooden seat and porcelain bowl, and they will leave a far from zen-like atmosphere which subsequently causes you to hold your breath, light three candles and exit rapidly.

GET USED TO...

... the icy cold feeling of porcelain on your bottom when you go to the loo in the dark of the night (not switching on the light, so as not to wake your darling man) and find that he has left the seat up. What's worse is when it is also wet.

... toe nail clippings in random places.

... finding that he has nearly finished the last packet of cereal, only to leave a smidgen in the box.

... being the social secretary. He will rely on you to remember every social engagement and all important dates, including your birthday, his siblings' birthdays and any anniversaries. You will also be responsible for the Christmas card list, naturally.

... balled socks under the bed whose cleanliness is suspect, at best.

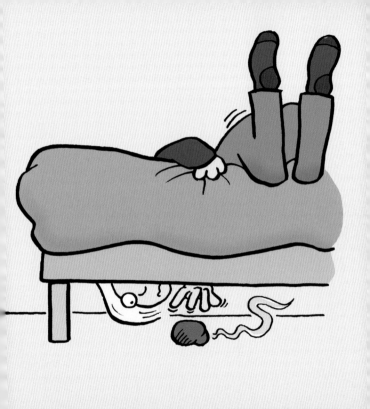

... talking to his mother/sister/ estranged relative, who only seems to phone when he is out and you would really rather watch *Love Actually*, which you rented in his absence.

... living in sin. Don't think that by living together you will be closer to getting married. Men view co-habitation as the ultimate stopgap. What is the point of getting married if you are living together anyway? Wouldn't you prefer to have a new kitchen rather than spend all that money on one Big Day?

HOME RULES

1. Cuddly toys do not get the best spot on the bed.

2. On a weekday morning, the bathroom sink should not be soaking 'delicates' unless you want them to be sprinkled with shaved stubble.

3. Don't complain about his bad breath if you expect him to kiss you when he wakes up.

4. The first person up makes the tea.

5. You are obliged to be at your partner's beck and call if they are sick. This is the living together perk for him. It is wrong to wish he were sick on a workday when you are out.

ADVANCED

DANGER ZONES

Don't compare yourselves unfavourably to the 'ideal couple' you know, who do everything together and are constantly, nauseatingly exhibiting public displays of affection. It will result in a lot of insufferable 'I told you so' glances from your undemonstrative partner when the perfect couple is the first to split up.

Weekends Away

If you are going away for the
weekend on your own, don't
come home early...

... all tidying up is done the
hour before you are due to
arrive back.

If the toilet is in the bathroom, you really don't want to be running a soothing bath with undertones of jasmine and lavender to relax in the morning after he went out for beers and a curry with the lads.

Friends

Friends can be shared, but note that in the event of a break up friends have to revert back to seeing only the one half of the couple they knew before. Therefore, any new friends gained have to be claimed for future ownership in case of this eventuality.

Things Not to Ask

🏠 Questions about The Future
– unless this is about what
is coming up at the movies,
where to go on holiday or what
to have for dinner.

🏠 'Why do you spend so much time playing computer games? Which do you love more: PlayStation or me?' His gut reaction answer in this situation might not be what you want to hear.

🏠 'What are you thinking?' He's not thinking anything. Really.

THE END

You know you have been living together too long when:

♠ you spend every Friday night at home with pizza and a film and the video shop guy treats you both like blood relatives.

♠ you buy clothes for him because you know you can also wear them slobbing around the house.

♠ you finish each other's...
... sentences.

♠ he finishes your rose-scented deodorant.

♠ you share a toothbrush – even the morning after a night out on the beers and vindaloo.

♠ you can see each other wandering around naked and don't feel the urge to have sex.

♠ a trip to Homebase is a good day out.

AFTERWORD

Living together is a challenge, but take comfort from the fact that many couples have lived together for years and some even recommend it. You'll get used to his toenail-chewing and the new bathroom fragrance. *He'll* realise how empty his life was without all that you bring to a home… like aromatherapy candles, romantic comedy videos and salad. Using the pointers in this book, both your lives will be enriched. It's a bit like baking: by mixing together the right romantic ingredients and following some basic household instructions you'll end up with something that's more delicious than what you started with. A word of warning, though – when the timer pings you may end up with a bun in the oven.